DARE TO DOODLE!

CAN YOU COMPLETE OVER 100 DRAWINGS AND LET YOUR PENCILS LOOSE?

BARRON'S

First edition for the United States and
Canada published in 2015
by Barron's Educational Series, Inc.

Published in 2015 by Carlton Books Limited
20 Mortimer Street, London W1T 3JW

Author: Caroline Rowlands
Illustrator: Eglantine Ceulemans
Design: Emma Wicks
Art Editor: Dani Lurie
Executive Editor: Anna Brett
Production: Marion Storz

All inquiries should be addressed to:
Barron's Educational Series, Inc.
250 Wireless Boulevard
Hauppauge, NY 11788
www.barronseduc.com

ISBN: 978-1-4380-0642-0

Date of Manufacture: December 2014
Manufactured by: Leo Paper Group
Printed in Heshan, China

9 8 7 6 5 4 3 2 1

Place a COIN under the paper and rub over it with the side of a **CRAYON.**

Keep going until the treasure chest is full.

It's MEERKAT MAYHEM down there.

Help these critters burrow up to the surface before the SNAKE catches them.

boulders = blockages

Add FLAMES to this fearsome, fire-breathing DRAGON.

Make sure your fingers don't get **munched.**

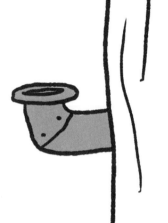

Do you have any ideas about what to DOODLE up here?

Try turning the book around and doodle in a submarine under the water.

Leave the
book this way
up and doodle
some scary sea
monsters, lurking
deep
deep
down...

What's the scariest thing you've ever run away from?

CLOSE YOUR EYES
and keep doodling sticks
until you think you've built these
birdies a (very messy!) NEST.

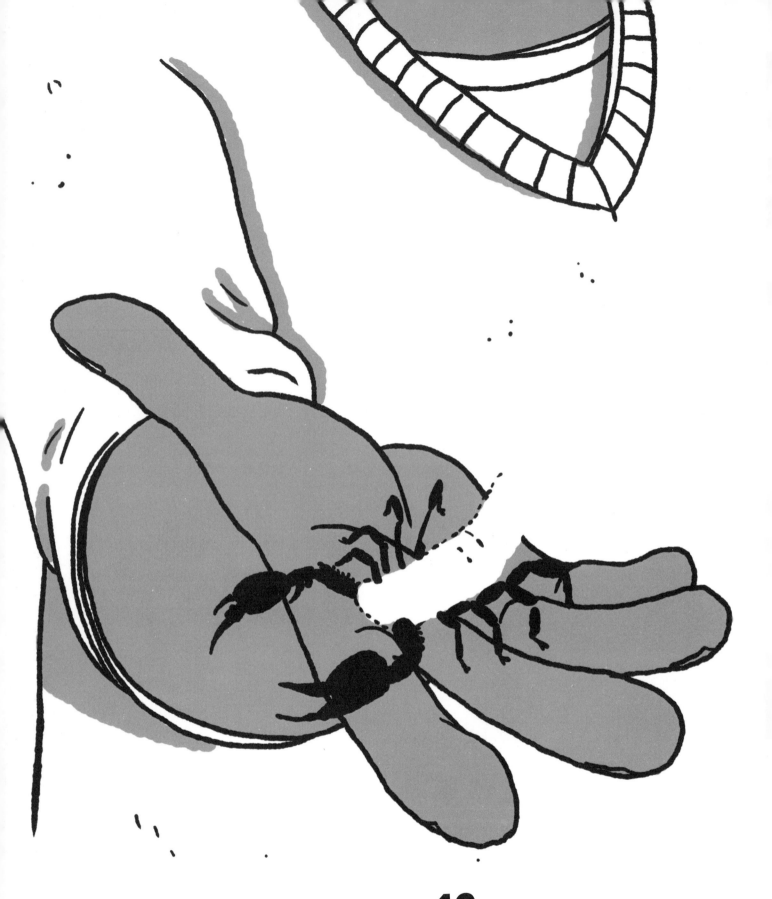

Dare you to **hold** this scorpion for **10** seconds!

Watch out for the poisonous tail!

Can you create a doodle LADDER?

Start with one doodle, and turn it into something else by the time you reach the top of the ladder.

START HERE

What do you see? A DUCK... or a RABBIT?

Doodle some more pictures that look like one thing... and then something else!

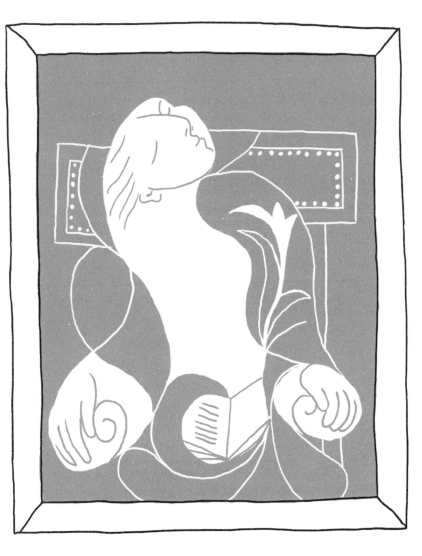

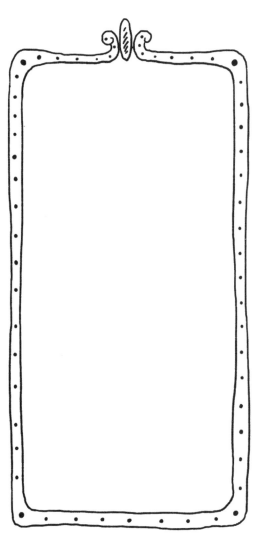

Have you ever seen a work of art and just wanted to doodle all over it?

Go on... I dare you...

YOUR MISSION:

Doodle these rocket ship parts in the right order to BLAST OFF to the moon. 10...9...8...7...

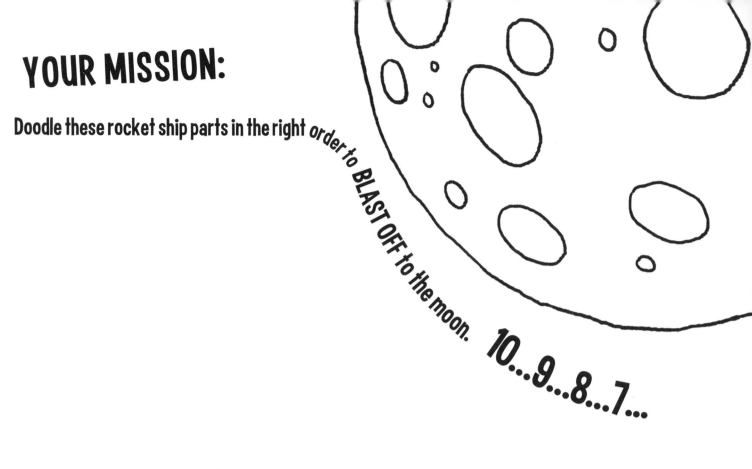

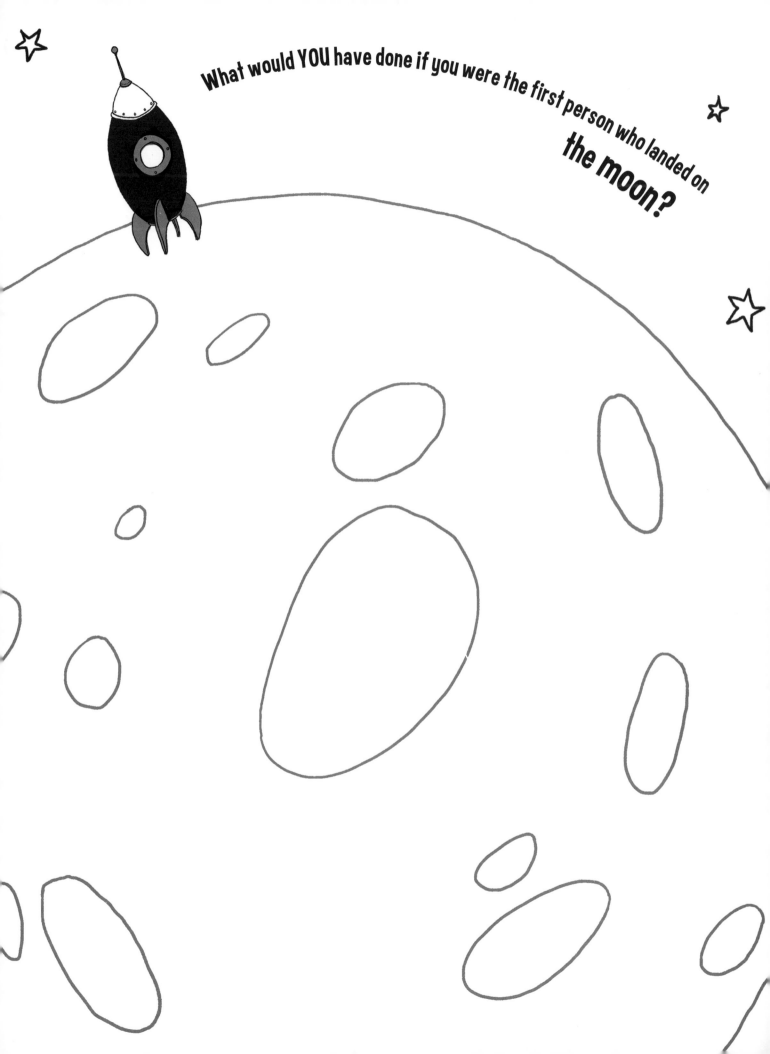

What would YOU have done if you were the first person who landed on **the moon?**

DOODLE A FROG IN THREE EASY STEPS...

How many frog doodles can you squeeze onto this lily pad?

I guess... ___ frogs

I actually doodled... ___ frogs

HOP onto the next page...

Doodle some more frogs in the spaces along the log.
Cut along the dotted lines, then wrap each strip tightly around
your pencil to create a fly-swatting, twisty tongue for each frog.

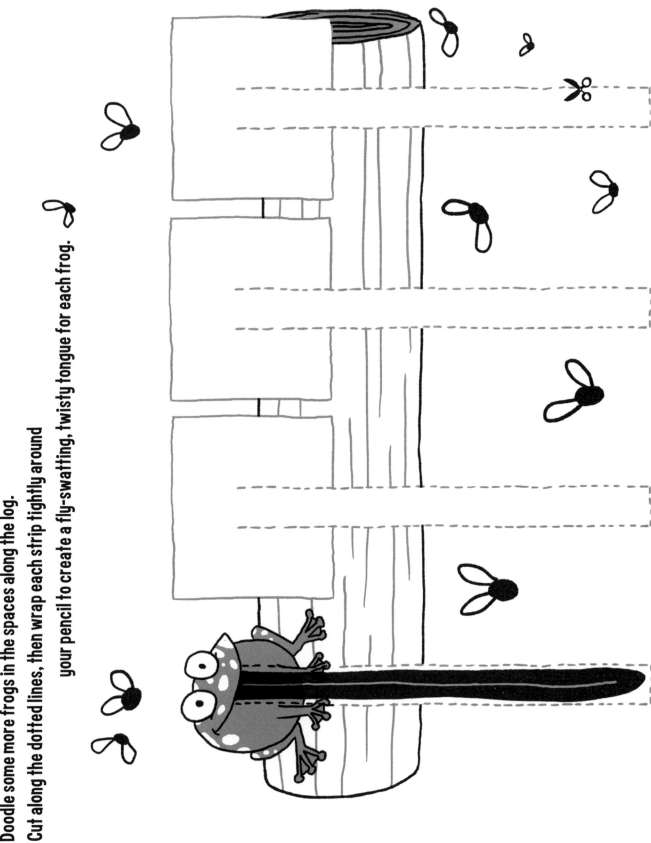

Imagine if you could leap onto TALL buildings in a single bound!

What kind of SUPERHERO would you be?

Doodle yourself and your superhero powers in action!

Doodle your superhero self saving the day in your very own comic strip story.

ONE DAY...

POW

ZAP

WHAM

THE END

Doodle your favorite foods on the meal coupons below, then cut them out and give them to your mom or dad when you want them for BREAKFAST, LUNCH, and DINNER!

WARNING! Before you cut—turn the page and fill in the doodles on the back of the coupons for double the fun!

Good for one meal	Good for one meal	Good for one meal
Good for one meal	Good for one meal	Good for one meal
Good for one meal	Good for one meal	Good for one meal
Good for one meal	Good for one meal	Good for one meal
Good for one meal	Good for one meal	Good for one meal
Good for one meal	Good for one meal	Good for one meal

1. Keep DOODLING this stick figure in lots of different positions (one in each box).
2. CUT the boxes out and put them in a pile.
3. Hold the pile by the left edge and pull all the boxes back, so you're looking at the bottom of the pile.
Then FLIP them back and they'll show your stick figure in motion.

CAN YOU CHANGE THE FEATURES ON THESE FACES TO MAKE THEM LOOK...

HAPPY
SAD
angry
SICK
scared
embarrassed
mischievous
sleepy
surprised

Ready...
aim...
fire!

Close your eyes and see if you can draw a line from each of the arrows to the targets on the opposite page.

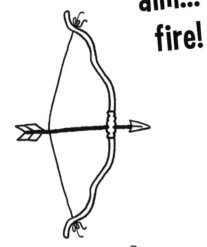

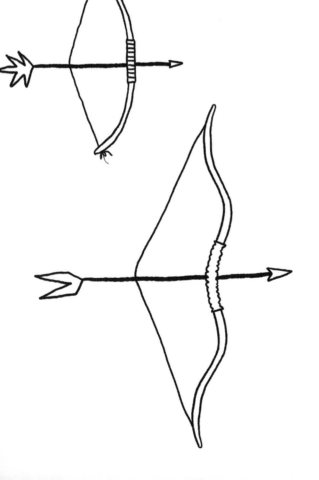

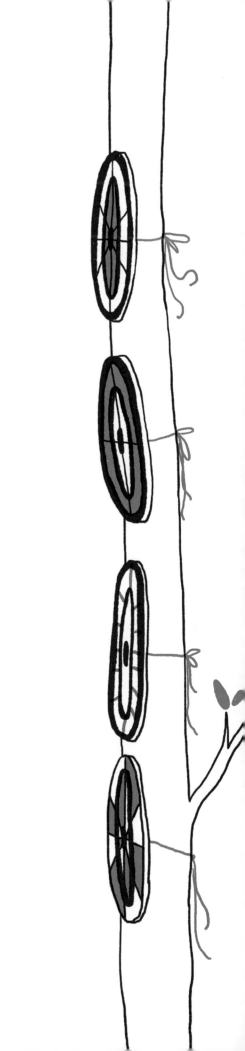

Grab your skis and start doodling down this MOUNTAIN.

Look again! Now what do you see? HIGH mountains or HUGE waves?

Grab your surfboard and get doodling.

**Fill up
the page
with this
BRICK
pattern.**

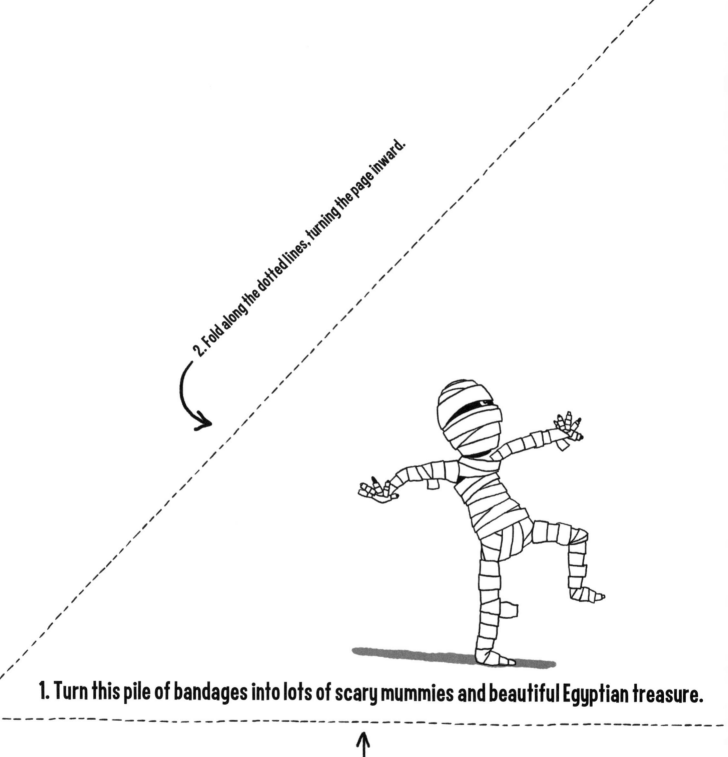

2. Fold along the dotted lines, turning the page inward.

1. Turn this pile of bandages into lots of scary mummies and beautiful Egyptian treasure.

3. Don't doodle anything below this line.

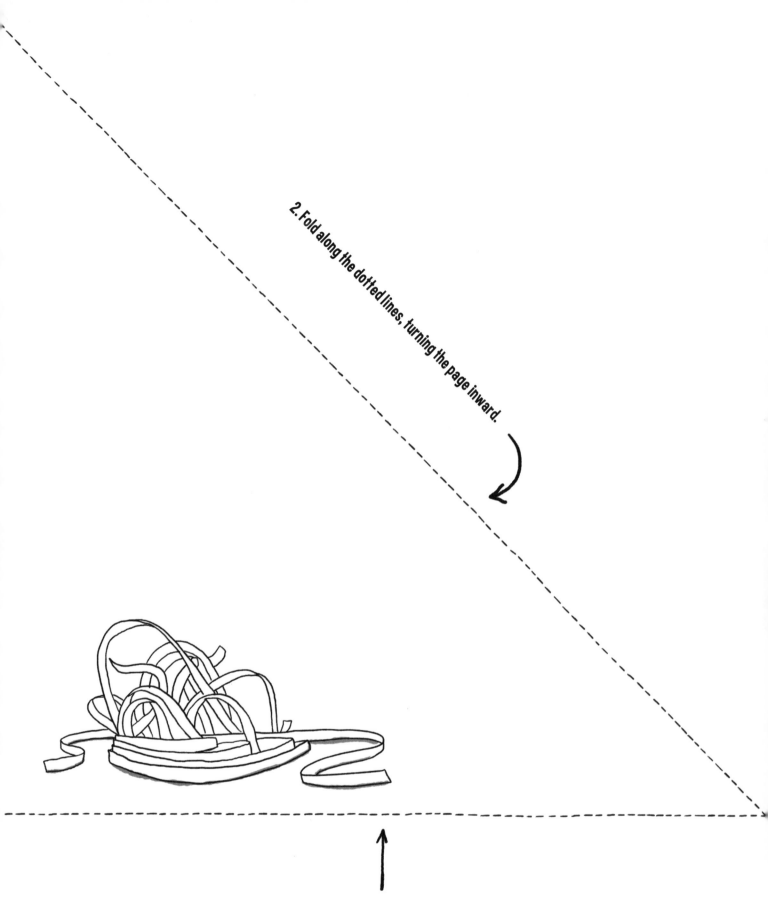

2. Fold along the dotted lines, turning the page inward.

4. Doodle some more bricks on the folded page above
to keep the mummies trapped inside the pyramid!

Add some more hieroglyphics to the pyramid.

Play your favorite song, **close your eyes,** and doodle the first thing that pops into your mind.

Turn these ink SPLATS into some funny doodles.

Add a rope ladder, some branches, and a trunk to turn this HOUSE into a cool TREEHOUSE.

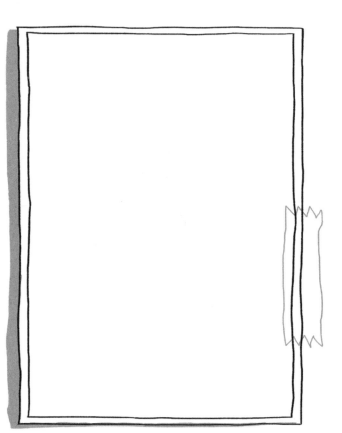

...your best friend is doing right now!

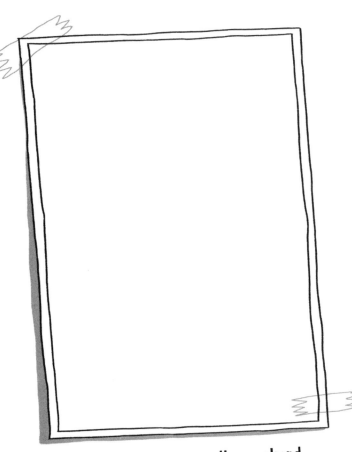

...your teacher does on the weekend.

...your bedroom would look like with all
your stuff stuck to the ceiling.

...you will look like when you grow up.

What do you think this boy sees through his **BINOCULARS?**

Follow the instructions to figure out where to doodle the buried treasure on the map.

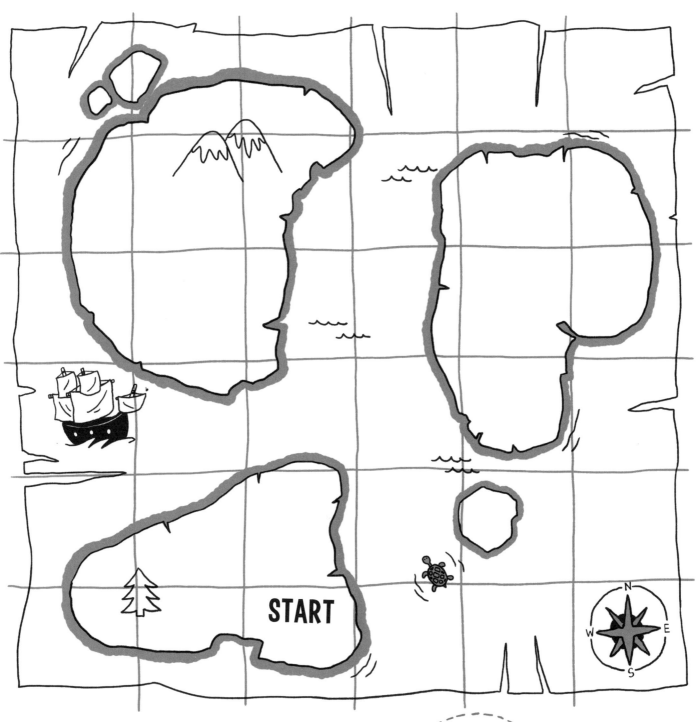

START

Sail EAST 3 squares.

Sail NORTH 2 squares.

Get off your ship and travel WEST 1 square.

Head SOUTH 1 square.

Sail WEST 1 square.

Venture NORTH 3 squares and WEST 2 squares...

That's it! Mark the spot with an X, or doodle whatever treasure you'd most like to find.

Now turn the page to find out what to do next...

1. Cut along the dotted line and remove this page from the book.

2. Ask a grown-up to make a cup of tea and pour it into a bowl.

3. When the tea has gone cold, put your map in the bowl and leave to soak for a couple of hours.

4. Remove and leave to dry for the most authentic treasure map EVER!

Draw some lines to finish the top of this stable door. Then cut along the dotted line and open the top door.

NOW OPEN THE BOTTOM DOOR.

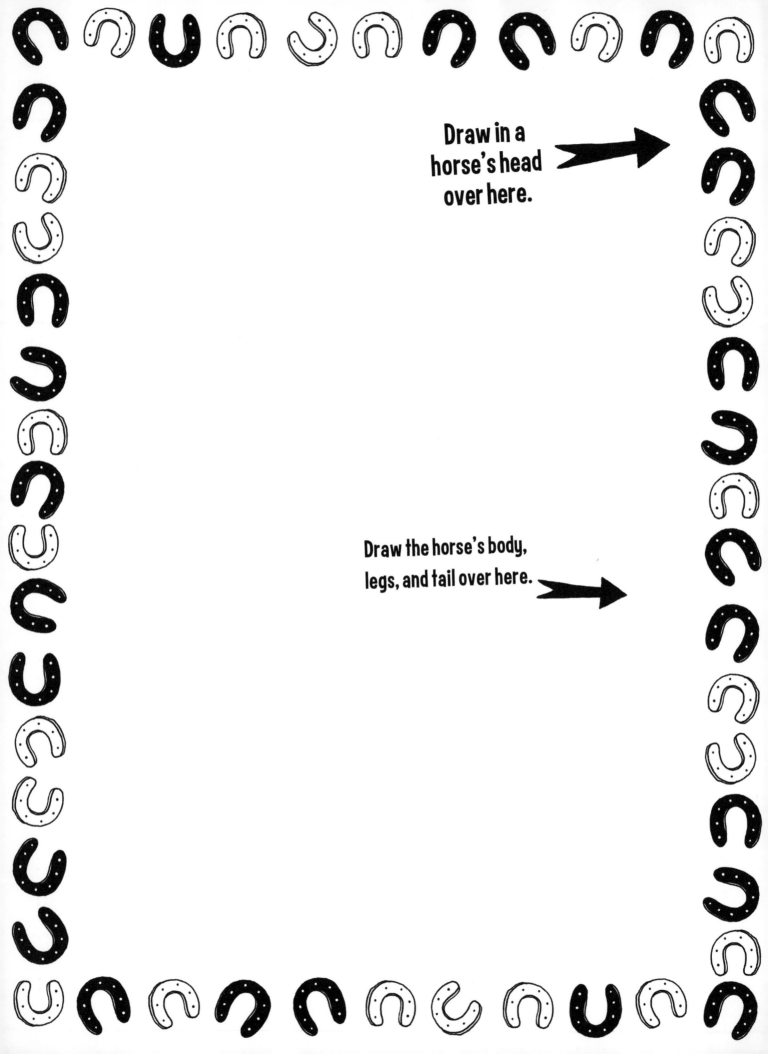

Draw in a horse's head over here.

Draw the horse's body, legs, and tail over here.

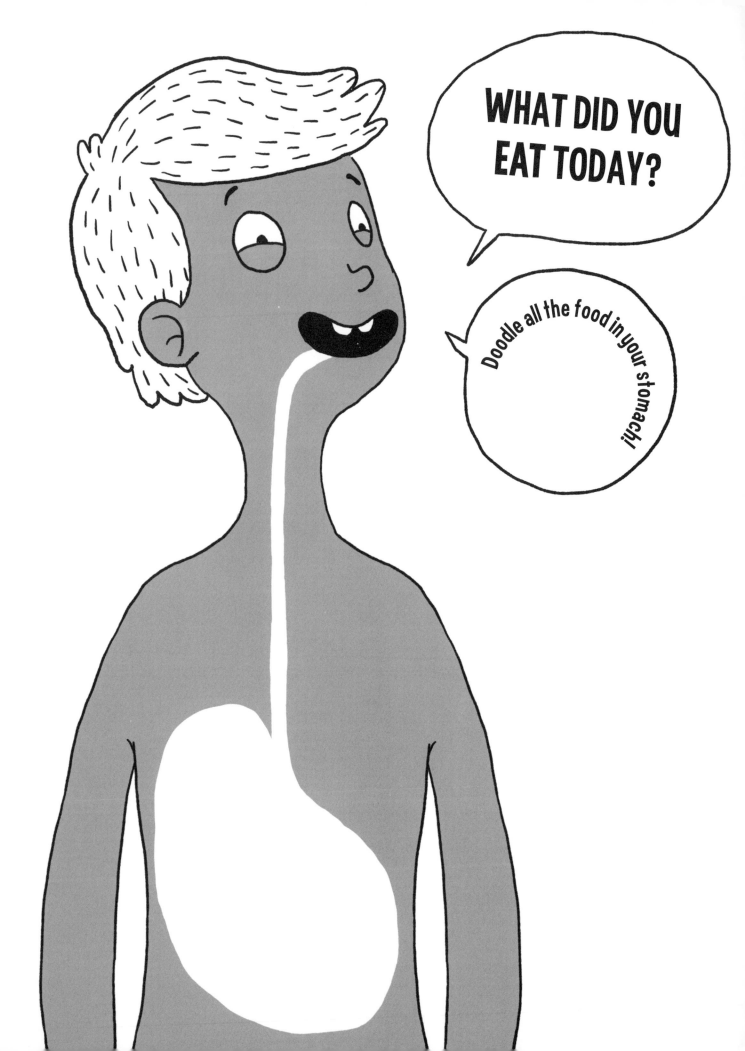

Look very closely at these matchsticks.

Can you doodle three of these matchsticks in the same position, and move one matchstick to make a square?

Answer on the next page.

Tick *tock* ...it's doodle o'clock!

Instead of numbers, doodle what YOU do each hour on the clock.

This is the answer to the matchstick puzzle on the previous page! If you move the match on the left out slightly, it will create a small square in the middle of all the matchsticks. Clever!

Abracadabra...   AL-A-GA-ZANG!

Make some white rabbits
magically appear...

With a **whizz** and a **BANG**.

There are more stars in the universe than grains of sand on all the beaches on Earth!
See if you can spot some famous constellations by connecting the dots.

BIG DIPPER

HERCULES

ORION

CANIS MAJOR

Is anyone out there?

Turn these wiggly lines into some funny aliens.

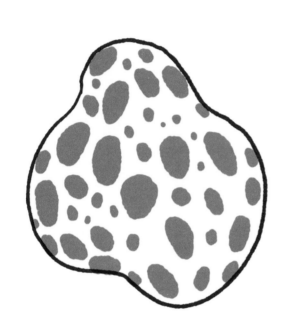

Which way UP?

Create some doodles that look the same, any way you look at them.

This way up.

No, this way up.

No, this way up.

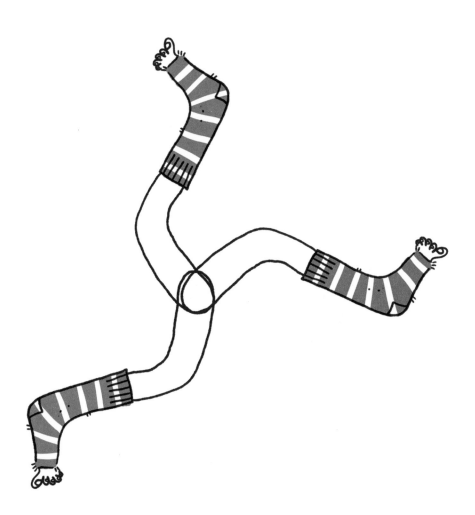

Now try this way up.

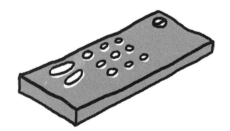

Dotty about doodles?

Prove it by creating some cool drawings using only spots and dots.

Can you think of **TEN** things that FLY?
Write them here, then see if you can draw them in **TWO** minutes.

1. _____
2. _____
3. _____

4. _____
5. _____
6. _____
7. _____

8. _____
9. _____
10. _____

Now think of TEN things that float.

Write them here, then see if you can doodle them all in 60 seconds.

.1 _____   4 _____   .8 _____

2 _____   5 _____   9 _____

3 _____   6 _____   10 _____

.7 _____

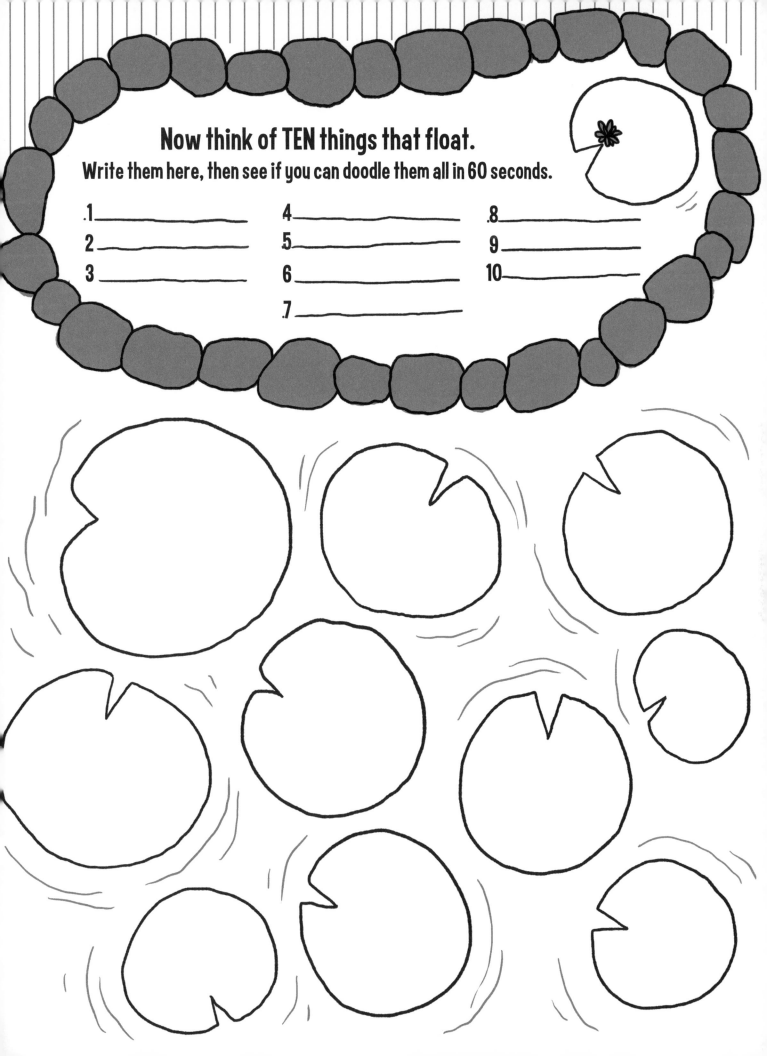

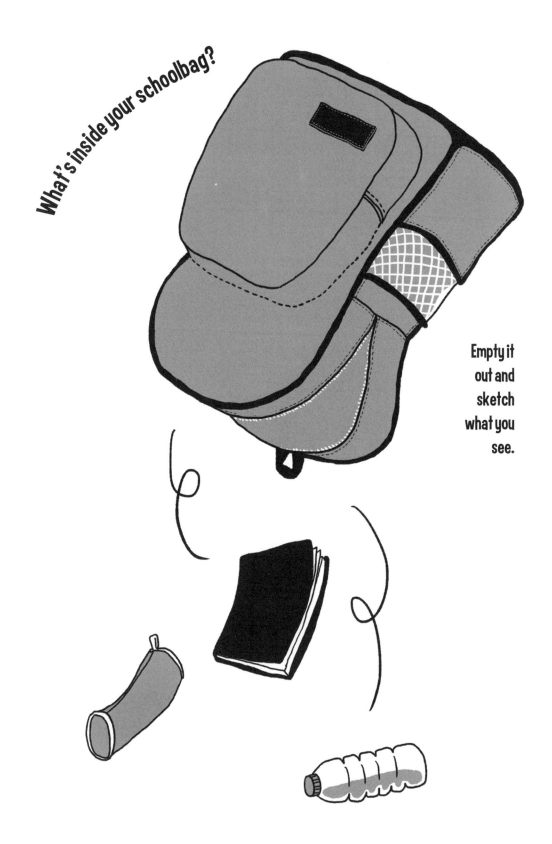

What's inside your schoolbag?

Empty it out and sketch what you see.

If you could add one item, what would it be?

Do you ever look at something and see it DIFFERENTLY than everyone else does?

Turn these everyday objects into something DOODLE-TASTIC!

Turn your book around.

Top deck or bottom deck—where do you like to sit on a bus?

Doodle yourself on the bus with your friends.

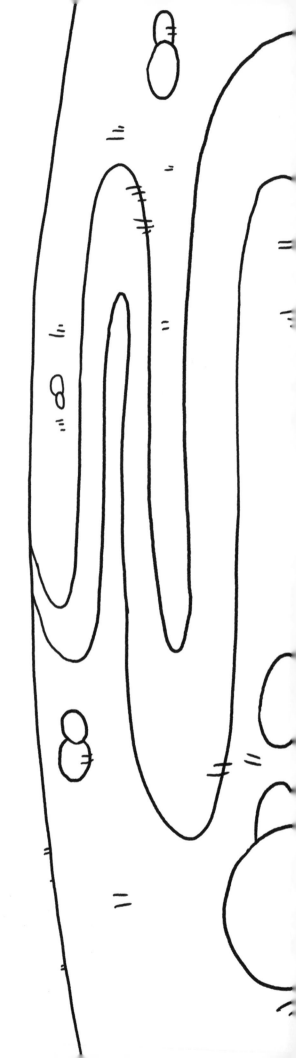

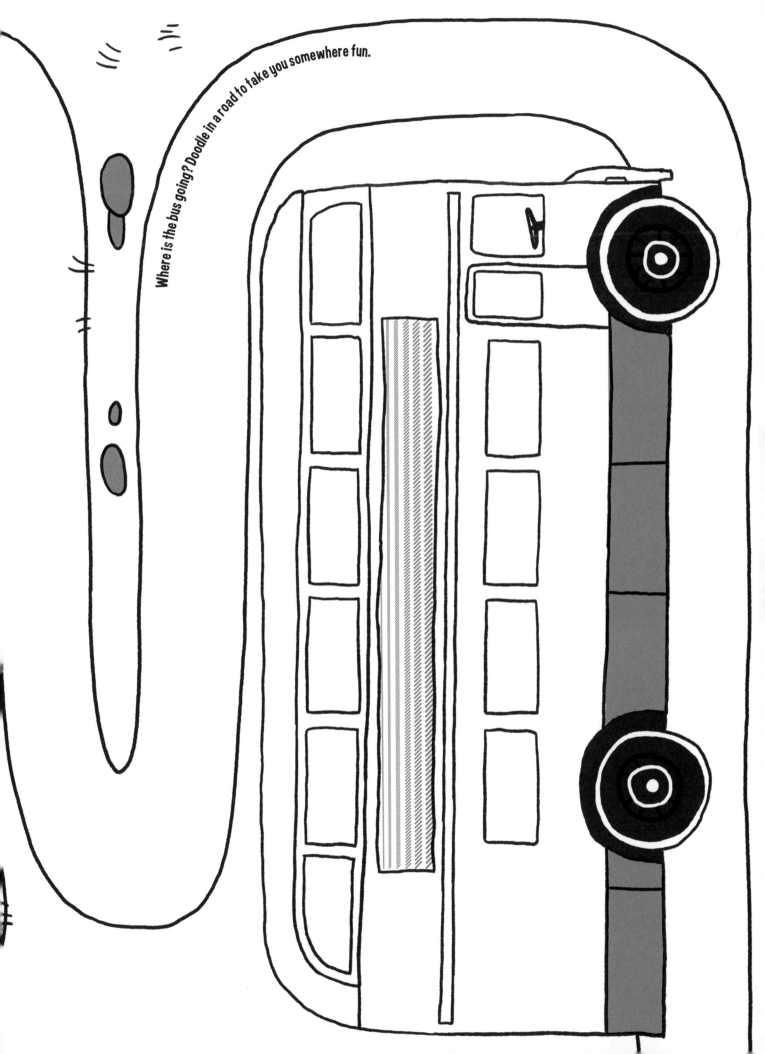

Where is the bus going? Doodle in a road to take you somewhere fun.

DOODLE your initials and fill them with doodles all about you.

What you like...

what you eat...

what you do...

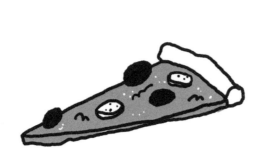

Want to make a mess?

Blob some splats of paint onto this page.

Blow through a straw to spread the paint to make as much mess as you can.

Wait for the paint to dry, then add some doodles to turn your mess into a masterpiece!

How many different kinds of ROBOTS can you create, using just these parts?

What goes in...

Doodle them on the conveyor belt.

Then create a design on the toy boxes to package the robots in.

Start here

Use this page to create the **WILD WILD WEST**.

Doodle a cowboy on his horse and chase down the runaway train.

Yee-HAW!

Scare away the crows with a
dingle-dangle-doodle-tastic SCARECROW.

Doodle some veggies in the soil for this farmer to harvest.

Doodle in the utensils the chef needs to make some delicious
PIZZAS.

MENU

WHAT ARE YOUR FAVORITE PIZZA TOPPINGS?

Make the cavemen feel at home and decorate their cave with some prehistoric art.

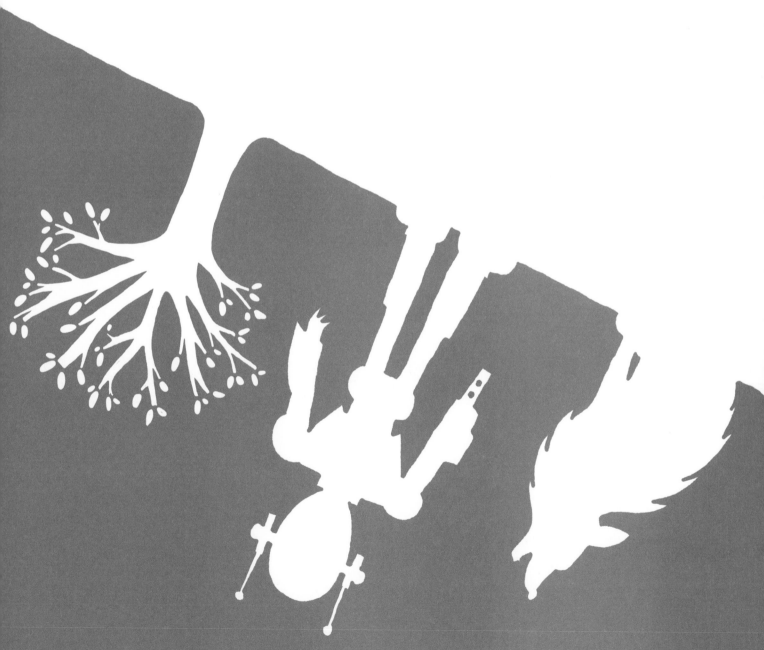

Can you doodle a drawing that really stands out? **HERE'S HOW...**

1. Trace your hand and wrist.

2. Go over it with a dark pen, adding curves to highlight where the hand and fingers are.

3. Use a thicker, darker color to go over seven or eight of the lines across your hand.

4. Add bright colors around the dark outline to make the hand really **stand out.**

S.O.S!

Can you doodle five ways to save the castaway on the desert island?

Watch out for the shark!

Imagine you could fly,
way up high.

Soar into the sky and doodle your hometown
way down below.

Time to turn the book around!

Doodle some funny faces in the circles below.
You'll find out why later.

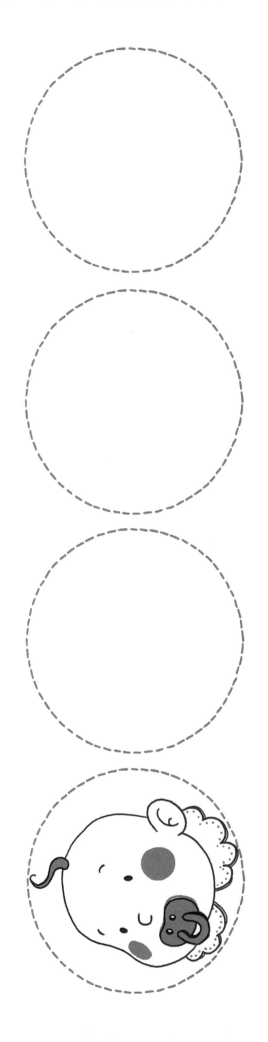

Use this page to doodle everyone you know.

Friends, family, teachers...

Dare you to make them look weird
with some crazy hairstyles and
wacky outfits.

THEN...
Fold down this page along
the black dotted line.

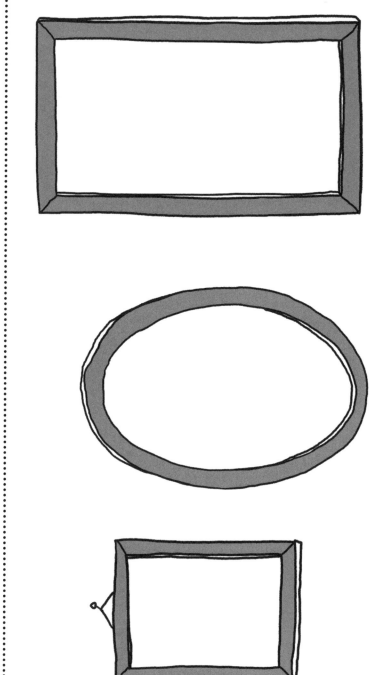

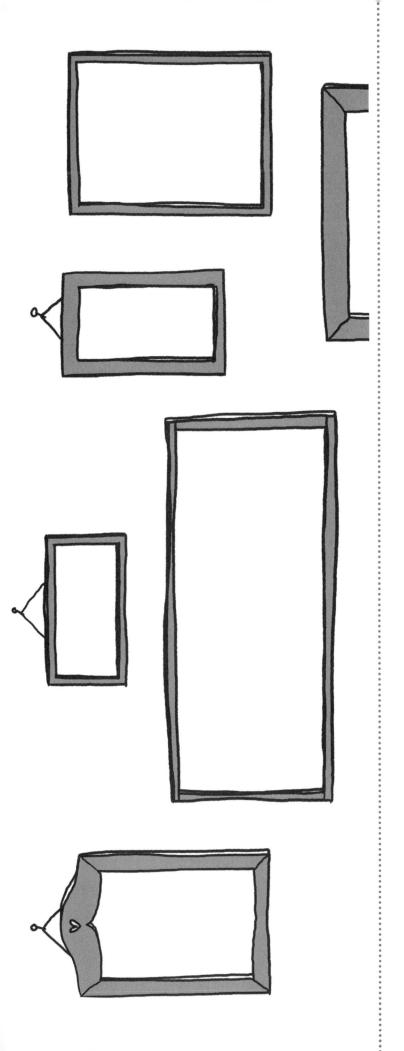

NEXT...
Fold up this page along the GREEN dotted line,
then doodle some bodies in the squares.

Draw yourself winning a game

of your favorite sport.

Now doodle some funny legs in the squares.

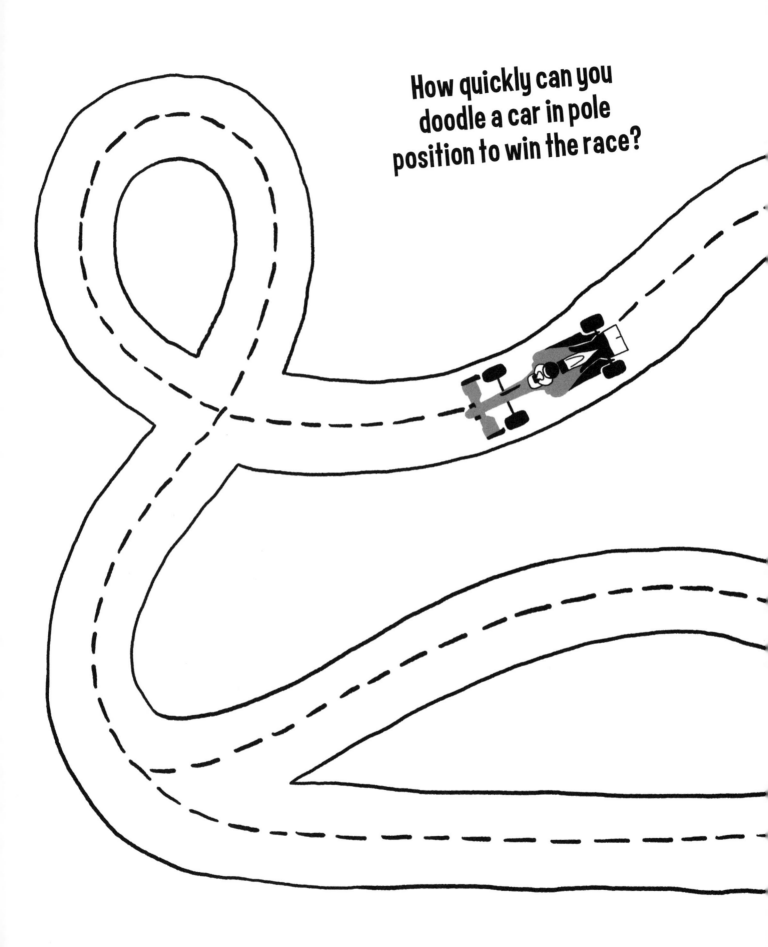

How quickly can you doodle a car in pole position to win the race?

ON YOUR MARKS...
GET SET...
GO!

Flip the book this way around.

Doodle some cheeky monkeys at the end of these curly tails.

Have you ever been in a haunted house?

Are you brave enough to cut along the dotted line and open the door? Get ready to doodle the scariest thing you can think of behind it.

Creep upstairs and downstairs and doodle in EIGHT more things that give you goosebumps.

BOO!

Pick your three best dino doodles and draw them again, this time inside the **TIME MACHINE.**

Doodle the DINOS as they TRAVEL through time.

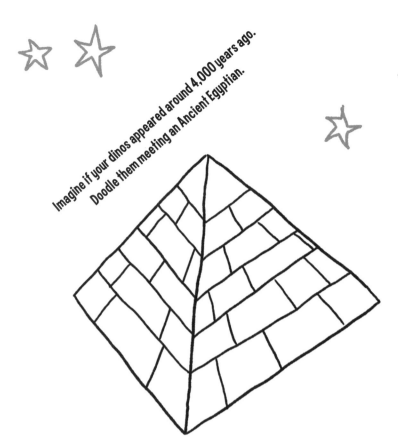

Imagine if your dinos appeared around 4,000 years ago.
Doodle them meeting an Ancient Egyptian.

Imagine your dinos battling it out in a CASTLE siege.
Quickly arm them with some bows and arrows.
Ready, aim, fire!

Yikes, it looks like they've landed on the **moon.**

Uh oh! They're here. Right now!
In your BEDROOM... and jumping
up and **down** on your bed!

Doodle this straw.

Get a glass of WATER
and a STRAW
(or a pen if you can't find a straw).

Stand the straw in the
glass of water. Does the
straw look straight?

**Doodle what
you can see.**

Now doodle what you think it would look like in a glass of water.

COOL SCIENCE! The straw looks
like it bends because you are
looking at it through different
mediums—water and glass. This
is called REFRACTION.

Why did the chicken cross the road?

To get to the other side.

Ha HA!

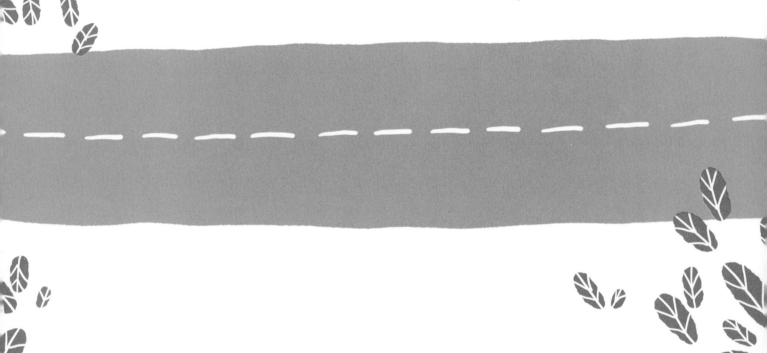

Can you doodle five different reasons why this chicken is crossing the road?

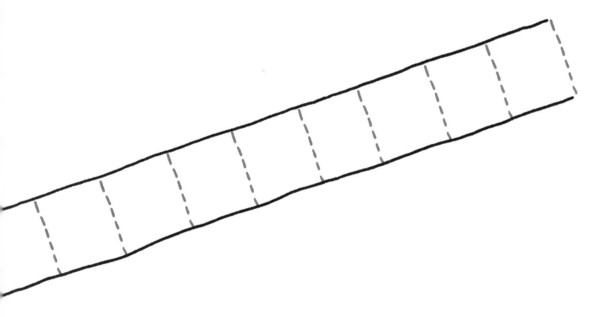

1. Doodle a monster's head, body, and legs in the middle of the page.

2. CUT along the dotted lines and fold back and forth along the dashed lines to create POP-UP MONSTER ARMS!

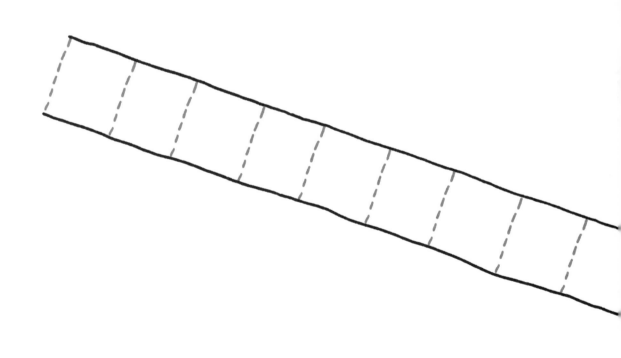

Go on, give him a HUG!

You've had enough HUGS, but your MONSTER wants more.
Doodle yourself running away from him.

How are you going to **escape?**

During your lifetime, you will spend about **SIX YEARS** dreaming!

What did you dream about LAST NIGHT?

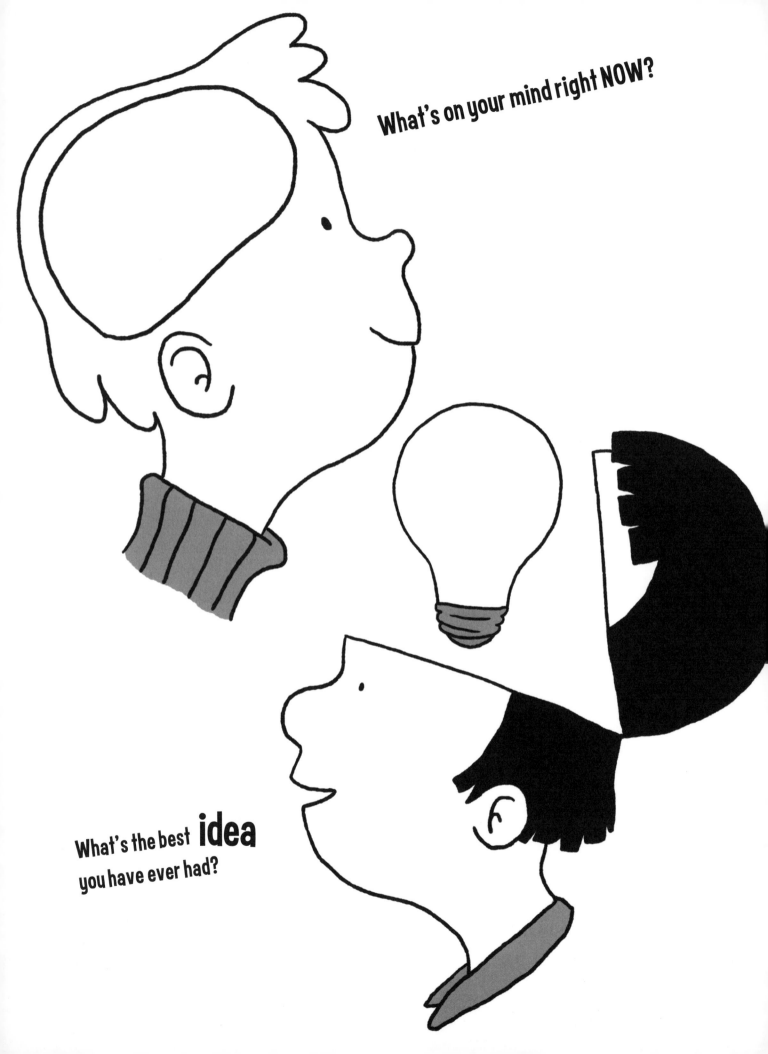

How many snowmen can you doodle in 60 seconds?

Your time starts...

NOW!

TAKE ONE FINGERPRINT.

Add some wiggly and straight lines.

Add another fingerprint.
(or even a thumb or toeprint)

And create lots of crazy doodles all over the page.

You'll need to turn the book around to recreate this picture of a GIANT.

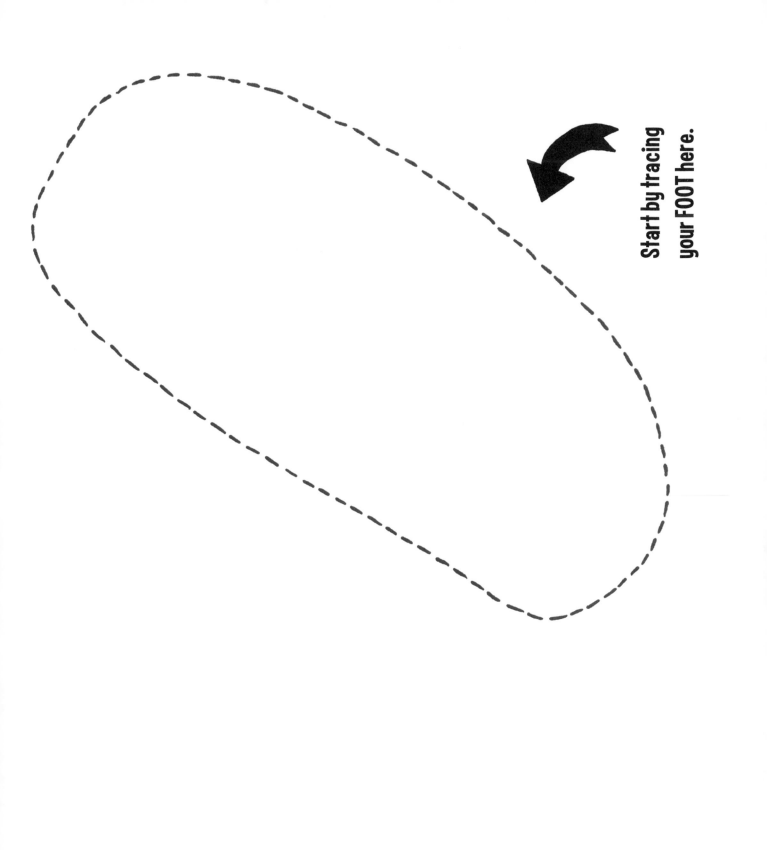

Start by tracing your FOOT here.

Show them a doodle of a dog, like the one below—made up of 11 straight lines and a dot for the eye.

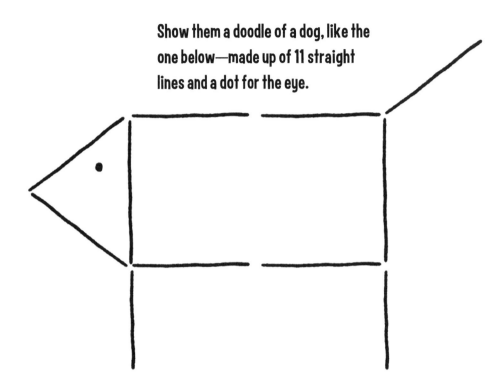

Ask your friend if they can doodle the dog looking in the opposite direction by moving just two of the lines (and the eye).

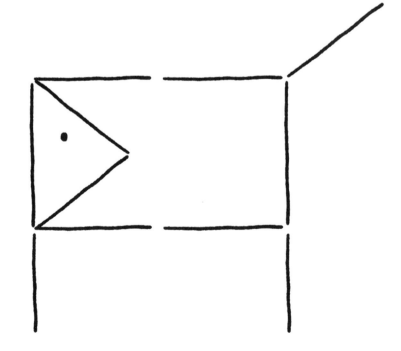

BET THEY CAN'T DO IT!

If you could **WIN** just one

TROPHY

in your lifetime...

WHAT would it look like?

WHY did you win it?

WHERE would you display it?

Doodle yourself and your four best pals at the top of this amazing waterslide.
Then figure out who slides to where, and doodle everyone making a BIG SPLASH at the bottom.

Turn this
page around.

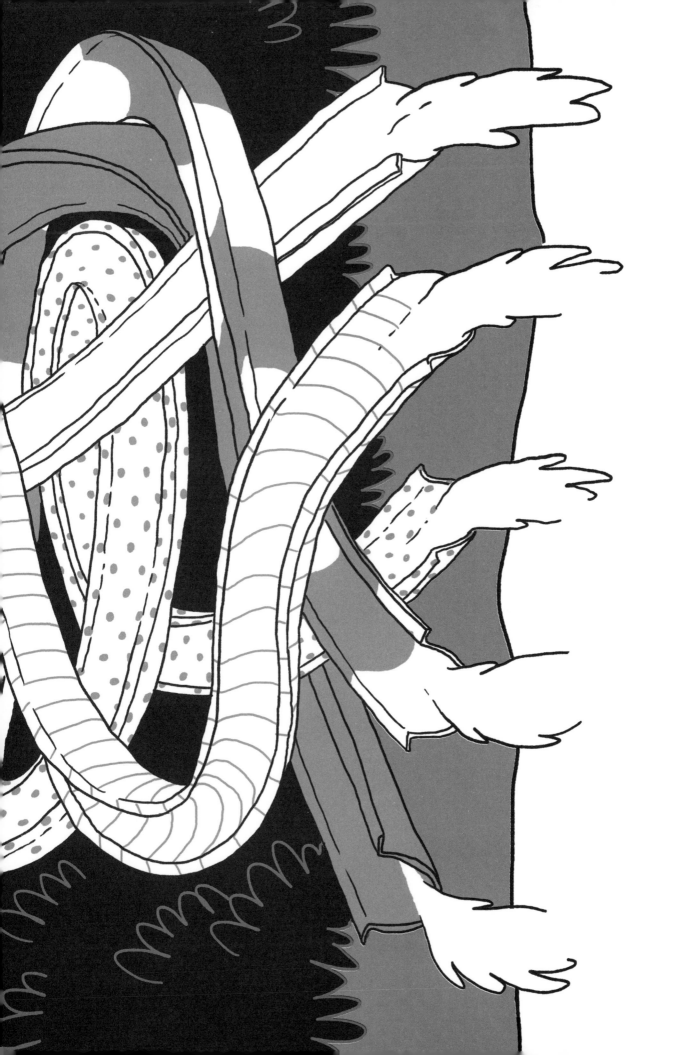

HAIRY SCARY!

Keep rotating the book around and around and doodle in some features so the beard becomes the hair and the hair becomes the beard.

Turn the book around.

Doodle a skateboarder defying **GRAVITY.**

WHAT HAPPENS NEXT?

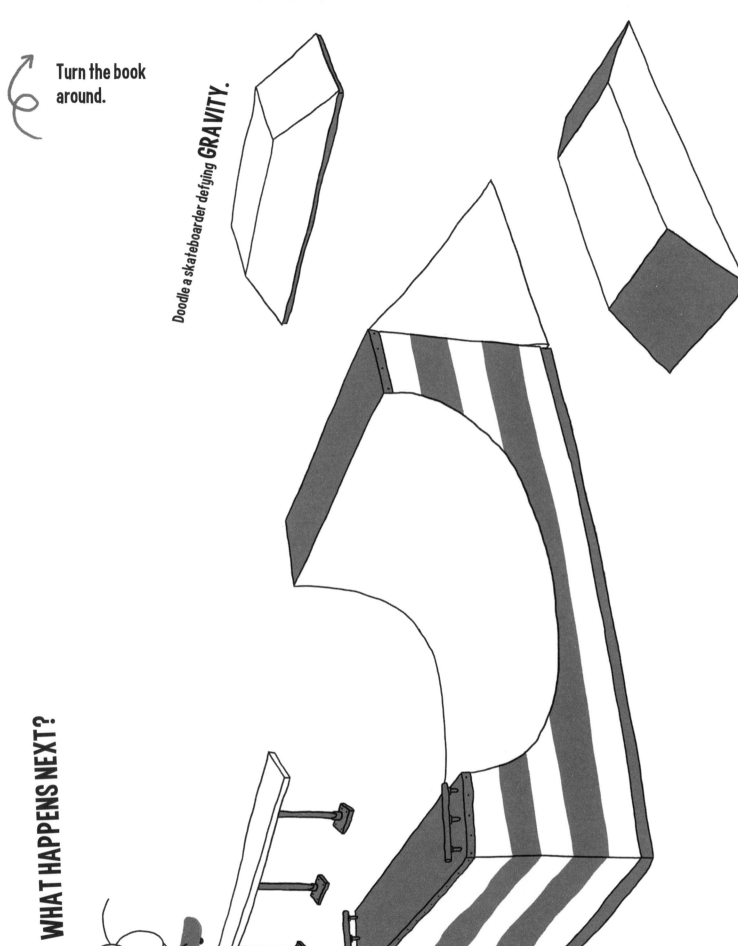

Are you brave enough to take a ride on the GHOST TRAIN?

Enter the dark tunnel and color everything **black...**

... except for the bubbles. Doodle some scary things in them to make you

SCREAM!

AAAArrrrrRRRrrrrrrrGGGGGGGGGGGGGGHHHHHHHHHHHHH!

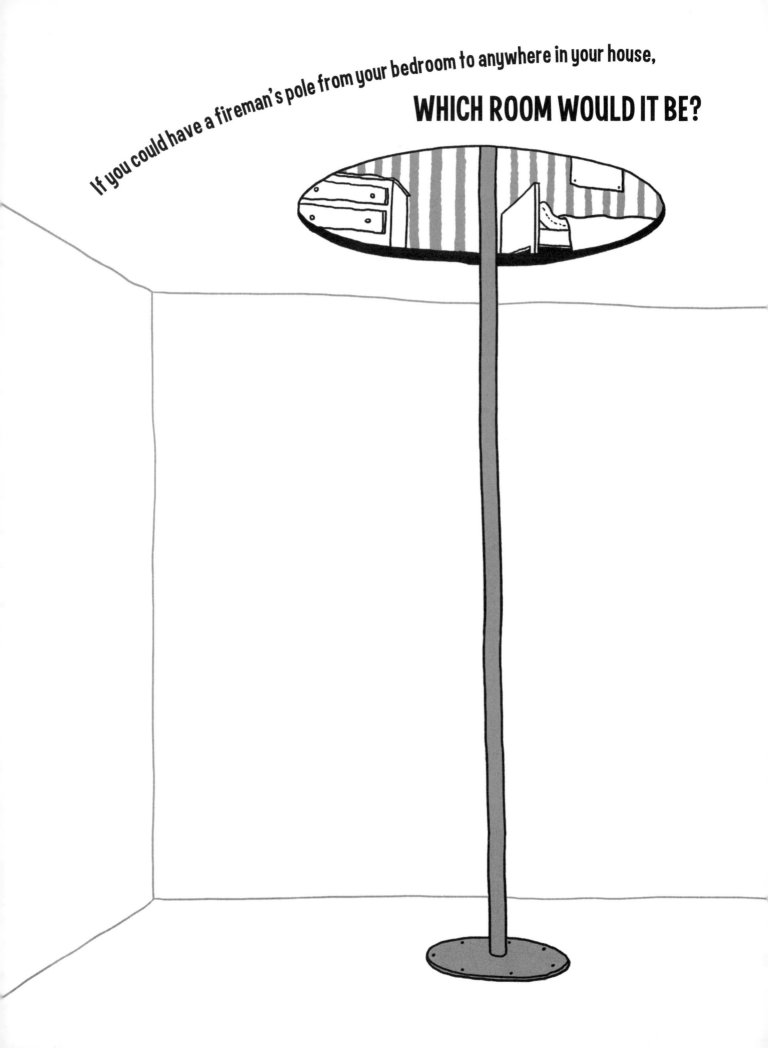

They're going to need a hose, a **LADDER,** and a **LOT** of **water!**

Turn the book this way.

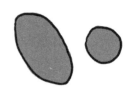

Doodle the bravest knight ever—ready to charge across the **drawbridge.**

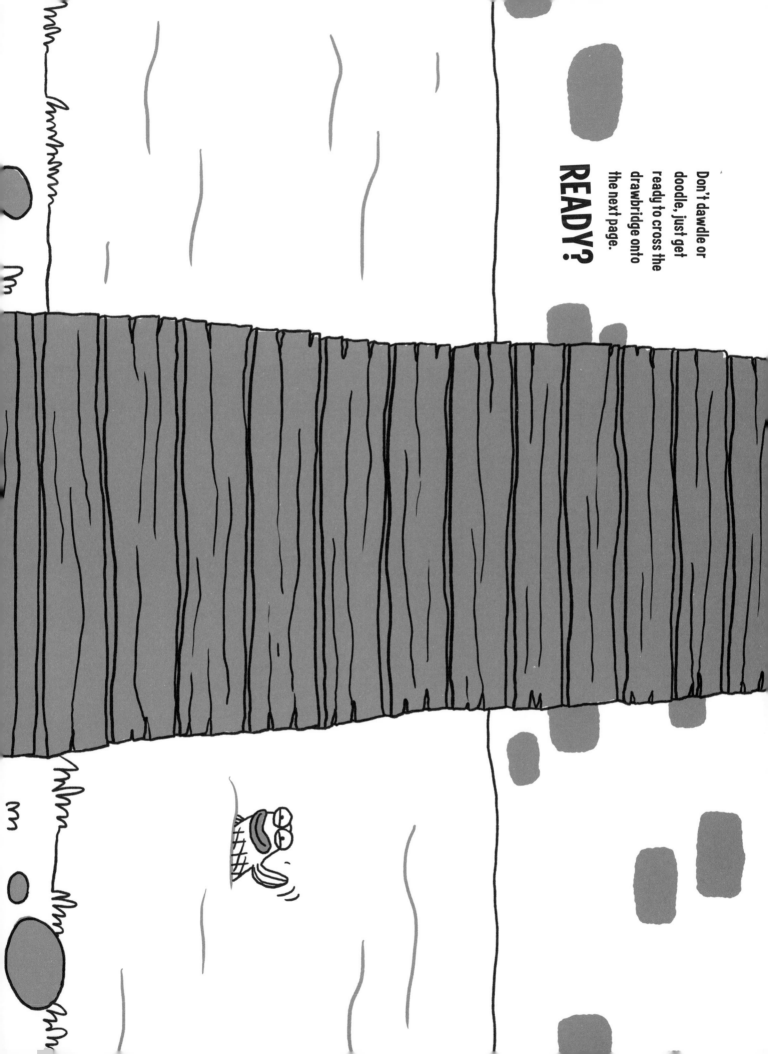

Don't dawdle or doodle, just get ready to cross the drawbridge onto the next page.

READY?

1. Doodle in the rest of the castle. Don't forget the arrow slits.

2. Fold here.

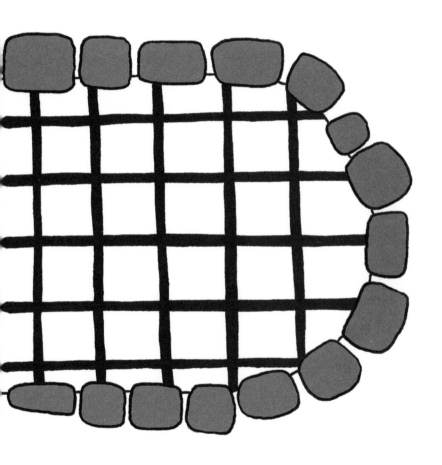

3. Cut along the dotted line. 4. Draw in some archers on top of the castle, ready to take aim and fire.

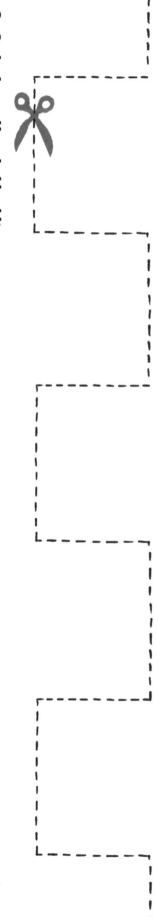

The battle has been fought and won. **HOORAY!**

Help the brave archers celebrate with a feast fit for a king.

Fill this page with snakes, more **SNAKES**, and nothing but **SNAKES**.

NOW COUNT THEM!

What do you like to do in the
OCEAN...

SURFING?

Floating lazily on a RAFT?

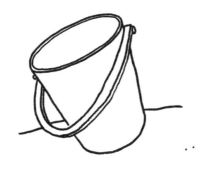

Hit the beach and doodle the best **SANDCASTLE** you have ever made.

Use your HANDS and a flashlight to create some SHADOW doodles.

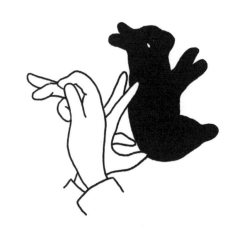

Create the most disgusting characters you can think of and cover them in even more disgusting, slimy **SNOT.**

DO YOU EVER JUDGE
A BOOK BY ITS COVER?

Find your favorite book and doodle its cover.

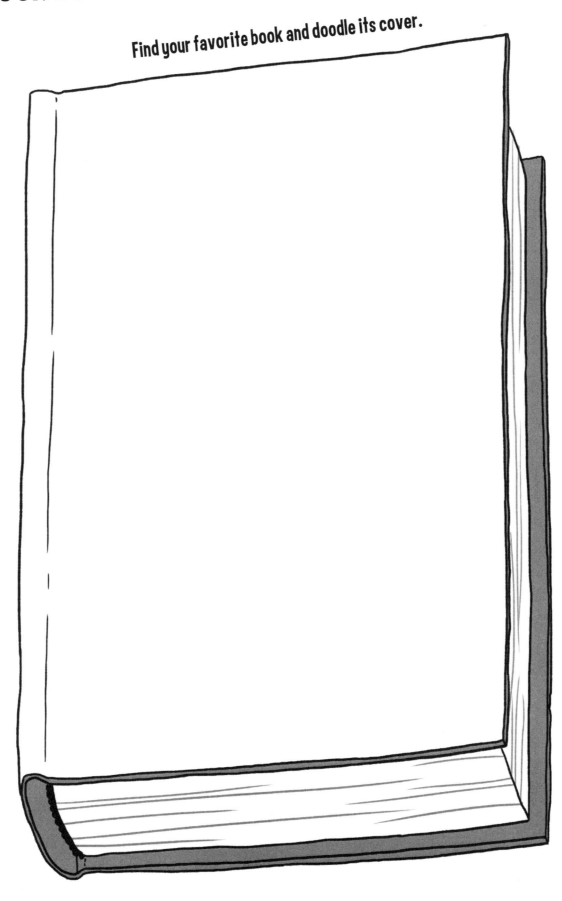

Now try the same doodle, but this time use your
OTHER HAND to do the drawing.

WHAT A CATCH!

Turn this fishing line into a fish...

then another doodle... then another doodle...

then another doodle...

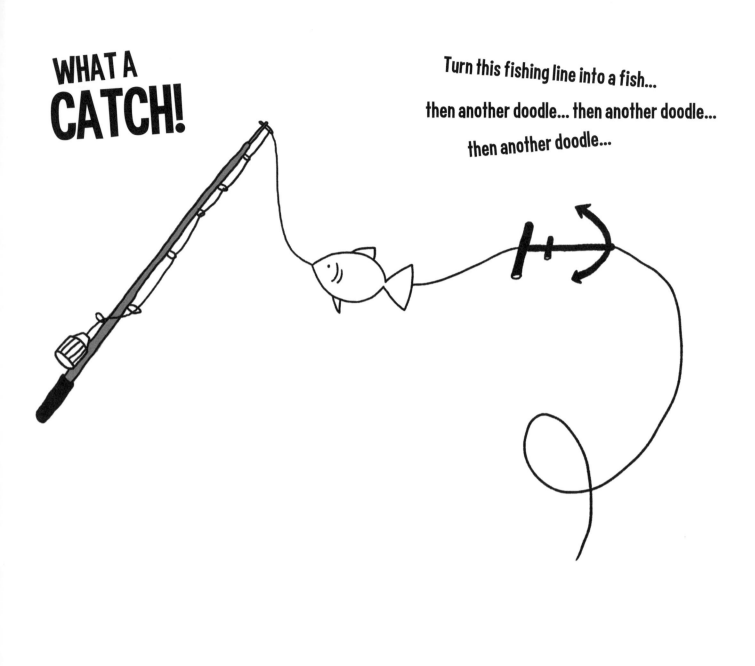

**Any good
at taking
PENALTIES?**

Close your EYES and see if you can shoot and SCORE
by doodling a line from the BALL TO THE GOAL.

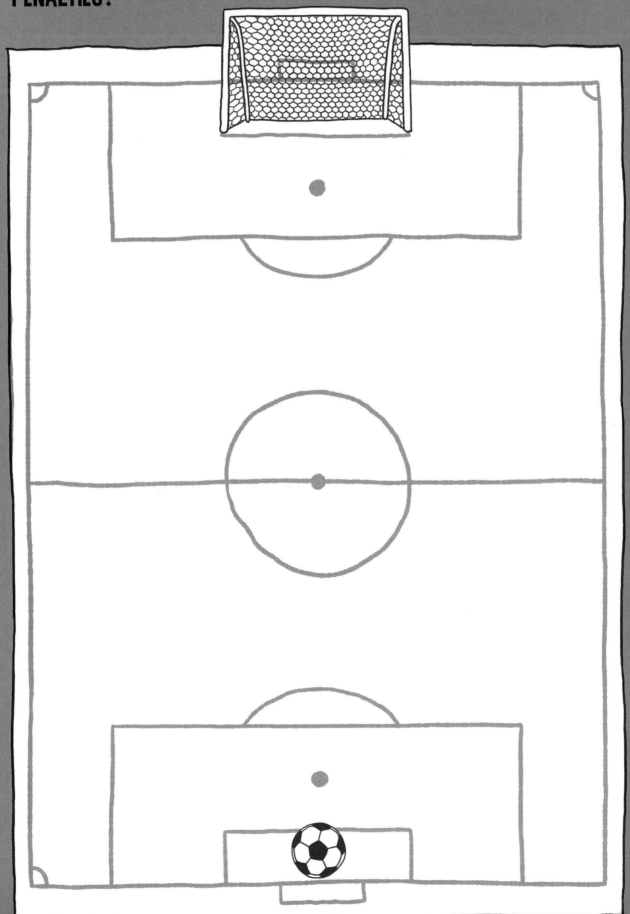

CAN YOU TURN THESE DOODLES INTO SOMETHING ELSE?

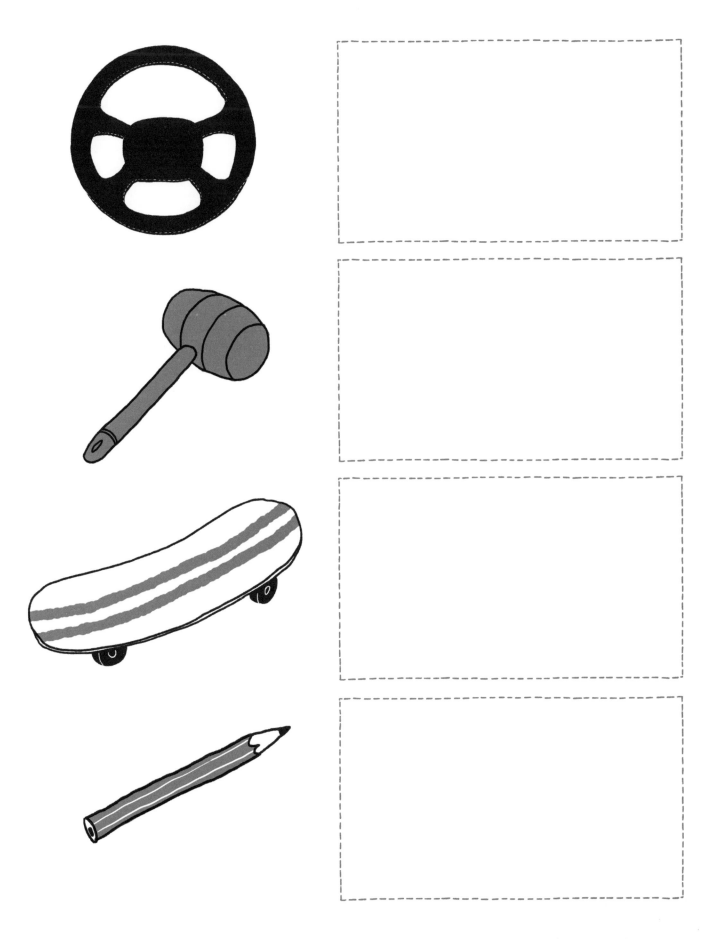

**When the going gets tough...
do you get going?**

What would you love to **CLIMB?**

What's the hardest thing you've ever dared to climb?

Doodle it here.

Look out of your BEDROOM WINDOW
before you go to sleep TONIGHT
and doodle what you can see.

FINAL CHALLENGE...

Can you go back to the start of the book and fit this character onto every page?